11+ Verbal Reaso

Standard Practice Paper
Pack Three 11A

Fill in your details:

Name..

Date of birth..

Male ☐   Female ☐

School...

Today's date...

Read these instructions before you start:

- You have **50 minutes** to complete this paper.
- There are 100 **questions** in this paper and each question is worth one mark.
- You may work out your answers in rough using the space around the questions.
- Make sure you write the answers very **clearly**.
- You will not lose marks for crossing out.
- Work as quickly and carefully as you can.
- If you find a question difficult, do **NOT** spend too much time on it but move on to the next one.

Moon Tuition
making the most of your potential

www.moontuition.co.uk

Section 1

In the following questions, move one letter from the first word to the second word without rearranging the letters to make two new words. These two new words must make sense. Write down the letter and two new words on the line provided.

Example

    pine   widow   _____

Answer

    n   (The two new words are **pie** and **window**.)

Question 1

    stow   election

    Answer: _____

Question 2

    fine   win

    Answer: _____

Question 3

    loose   fund

    Answer: _____

Question 4

    excited   rill

    Answer: _____

Question 5

supper   to

Answer: _____

Question 6

too   through

Answer: _____

Question 7

town   flow

Answer: _____

Question 8

health   ate

Answer: _____

Question 9

read   cot

Answer: _____

Question 10

node   quit

Answer: _____

Section 2

In the following questions, three of the five words in each group are related in some way. Underline the two words which are the "odd ones out ".

Example

white	red	keyboard	mouse	black

Answer

keyboard   mouse

Question 11

door	river	carpet	mountain	window

Question 12

rose	stalk	tulip	daisy	root

Question 13

water	food	juice	bread	milk

Question 14

rill	cloud	brook	stream	earth

Question 15

fierce	cub	cygnet	wild	lamb

Question 16

superior	small	minute	size	tiny

Question 17

scatter	force	disperse	meet	distribute

Question 18

merry	lean	slender	structure	thin

Section 3

In the following questions, a four letter word is hidden at the end of one word and the beginning of the next word. Underline the pair of words that contains the hidden word.

Example

All the cakes have been eaten.

Answer

been eaten(The hidden word is **neat**.)

Question 19

Tom found one book under the table.

Question 20

Lucy is looking for eggs.

Question 21

That widow never got married again.

Question 22

Have you hidden the cake?

Question 23

All yellow balls need to be put back in the box.

Question 24

Jessica keeps smiling today.

Question 25

This is her old bike.

Question 26

Do you have the receipt?

Question 27

Andrew likes playing with all his classmates.

Question 28

There is a dove near the bench.

Question 29

Is the tea still on sale?

Question 30

We need to find a way to motivate him.

Section 4

In the questions below, find two words, one from each group that are opposite in meaning. Underline both words.

Example

  (deceit real   trick)

  (actual size   artificial)

Answer

  real   artificial

Question 31

  (quiet huge quite)

  (sad   many loud)

Question 32

  (old   scatter odd)

  (run   even   fly)

Question 33

  (bold patient precious)

  (timid elated   dear)

Question 34

  (hide   show   take)

  (enlarge disclose small)

Question 35

  (vague full   relax)

  (tight   clear   far)

Section 5

In the following questions, letters stand for numbers. Calculate each sum and write down the answer as a letter on the line provided.

Example

If A=5, B=4, C=2, D=3 and E=8, then

A - B + C =_____

Answer

D

Question 36

If A=5, B=1, C=8, D=3 and E=0, find the answer to

this sum and write it as a letter.

(A+E) $\times$ B + D= _____

Question 37

If A=8, B=5, C=64, D=4 and E=13, then

C $\div$ A + B=_____

Question 38

If A=48, B=2, C=4, D=6 and E=1, then

A $\div$ D - B=_____

Question 39

If A=5, B=6, C=0, D=12 and E=18, then

(A + B) $\times$ C + D=_____

Question 40

If A=2, B=7, C=2, D=15 and E=14,then

(D - B) $\times$ A - C =_____

Question 41

If A=2, B=4, C=5, D=16 and E=1, then

$(B + D) \div B =$_____

Question 42

If A=3, B=4, C=9, D=8 and E=7, then

$B + D - C =$_____

Question 43

If A=49, B=1, C=6, D=8 and E=7, then

$A \div E - C =$_____

Question 44

If A=12, B=8, C=4, D=20 and E=3, then

$C \times B - D =$_____

Question 45

If A=4, B=6, C=8, D=3 and E=22, then

$D \times B + A =$_____

Question 46

If A=45, B=9, C=6, D=11 and E=8, then

$A \div B + C =$_____

Section 6

Work out the answer to each question using the given information.

Question 47

Andrew, Mark, Alex and Jack are good friends.

Alex is 2cm taller than Mark.

Andrew is 3cm taller than Mark.

Mark is 5cm shorter than Jack.

Who is the tallest?

Answer:_____

Question 48

Jane has twice as many sweets as Charlotte but she has four less than Lucy. Eunice has three more than Lucy.

If Eunice has nine sweets, how many does Charlotte have?

Answer:_____

Section 7

Use the alphabet below to work out the next pair of letters for each series. Write down the answer on the line provided.

A B C D E F G H I J K L M N O P Q R S T U V W X Y Z

Example

AO CP EQ GR IS (?)   Answer: KT

Question 49

BK EN HQ KT NW (?)   Answer:_____

Question 50

ZU AV BW CX DY (?)   Answer:_____

Question 51

RX TW VV XU ZT (?)   Answer:_____

Question 52

YY WB UE SH QK (?)   Answer:_____

Question 53

HA IZ JY KX LW (?)   Answer:_____

Question 54

MN OL QJ SH UF (?)   Answer:_____

Question 55

EG DF CE BD AC (?)   Answer:_____

Question 56

AB MN CD OP EF (?)   Answer:_____

Section 8

In the following sentences, three consecutive letters are missing from the word in capitals. The three letters spell a proper word without changing the order. Write the missing three-letter word on the line provided.

Example:

Anna **SPED** learning piano last month.

Answer:

TOP (The word in capitals is **STOPPED**.)

Question 57

Girls normally like going to PARS.

Answer:_____

Question 58

English sentences always begin with a ITAL letter.

Answer:_____

Question 59

Andrew and I went to the cinema TOHER.

Answer:_____

Question 60

How many ROOMS are there in your house?

Answer:_____

Question 61

More rain is ECAST for all areas.

Answer:_____

Section 9

In the following questions, write down the number that continues the sequence.

Example

    1   3   5   7   9   _____

Answer

    11

Question 62

    2   3   5   8   13   _____

Question 63

    3   6   12   24   48   _____

Question 64

    20   17   14   11   8   _____

Question 65

    1   2   4   7   11   _____

Question 66

    10   21   32   43   54   _____

Question 67

    2   5   8   11   14   _____

Question 68

    80   40   20   10   5   _____

Question 69

    5   10   20   25   35   _____

Question 70

    1   4   9   16   25 _____

Question 71

    1   1   2   3   5 _____

Question 72

    12   16   20   24   28 _____

Section 10

In the following questions, there are three pairs of words in the brackets. The second word in each of the first brackets has been formed using some of the letters from the first word. Find the missing word in the third bracket in the same way as the first two brackets. Write the answer on the line provided.

Example

    (begin   bin)   (below   bow)

    (throw   [?])

Answer

    tow

Question 73

    (blast   last)   (beach   each)

    (ahead   [?])

Answer: _____

Question 74

    (fold   gold)   (mail   nail)

    (late   [?])

Answer: _____

Question 75

    (teach   tea)   (rowing   row)

    (buyer   [?])

Answer: _____

Question 76

       (footwear   wear)   (foresee   see)

       (moreover   [?])

Answer: _____

Question 77

       (bicycle   cycle)   (reappear   appear)

       (trisector   [?])

Answer: _____

Section 11

A B C D E F G H I J K L M N O P Q R S T U V W X Y Z

In the following questions, words and codes are related in some way. Use the alphabet to help you work out the answer to each question.

Example

If the code for **SWAN** is **TYDR**.

What is the code for **TOOL**?

Answer

UQRP

Question 78

If the code for **HELP** is **IFMQ**.

What is the code for **MORE**?

Answer: _____

Question 79

If the code for **BROWN** is **DPQUP**.

What does **USIYT** mean?

Answer: _____

Question 80

If the code for **THERE** is **RFCPC**.

What is the code for **AMEND**?

Answer: _____

A B C D E F G H I J K L M N O P Q R S T U V W X Y Z

Question 81

If the code for **SWIM** is **TYLQ**.

What is the code for **RIVER**?

Answer: _____

Question 82

If the code for **EARLY** is **FCUPD**.

What does **QCSIW** mean?

Answer: _____

Question 83

If the code for **SPRING** is **RQQJMH**.

What is the code for **THOUGH**?

Answer: _____

Question 84

If the code for **ORCHID** is **MPAFGB**.

What does **MPYLEC** mean?

Answer: _____

Question 85

If the code for **MEMBER** is **NFNCFS**.

What is the code for **RESULT**?

Answer: _____

Section 12

In the following questions, the three numbers in each group are related in the same way. Find the number that fits in the last group in the same way as the first two groups. Write down your answer in the bracket.

Example

(4[9]5)   (11[13]2)

(3[   ]11)

Answer

14

Question 86

(7[21]14)   (8[17]9)

(30[   ]60)

Question 87

(90[10]9)   (32[4]8)

(42[   ]6)

Question 88

(4[24]8)   (6[26]7)

(15[   ]5)

Question 89

(30[10]20)   (36[24]12)

(50[   ]20)

Question 90

(54[9]6)   (144[12]12)

(60[   ]5)

Question 91

(20[14]8)   (12[10]8)

(30[   ]20)

Question 92

(16[14]2)   (20[8]12)

(50[   ]8)

Question 93

(10[50]60)   (10[90]100)

(12[   ]36)

Section 13

In the following questions, find a letter that can fit into both sets of brackets to complete the word before the bracket and begin the word after the bracket.

Example

    mea[   ]able

    rol[   ]ong

Answer

    l

Question 94

    tabl[   ]asy

    phon[   ]at   Answer:_____

Question 95

    wal[   ]ow

    sou[   ]ate   Answer:_____

Question 96

    ge[   ]eam

    foo[   ]old   Answer:_____

Question 97

    gues[   ]ilent

    bu[   ]tone   Answer:_____

Question 98

    che[   ]ind

    scar[   ]amily   Answer:_____

Question 99

jee[　]in

shee[　]ine　　Answer:_____

Question 100

ter[　]other

swi[　]ean　　Answer:_____

11+ Verbal Reasoning

Standard Practice Paper
Pack Three 11B

Fill in your details:

Name...

Date of birth..

Male ☐   Female ☐

School...

Today's date...

Read these instructions before you start:

- You have **50 minutes** to complete this paper.
- There are 100 **questions** in this paper and each question is worth one mark.
- You may work out your answers in rough using the space around the questions.
- Make sure you write the answers very **clearly**.
- You will not lose marks for crossing out.
- Work as quickly and carefully as you can.
- If you find a question difficult, do **NOT** spend too much time on it but move on to the next one.

Moon Tuition
making the most of your potential

www.moontuition.co.uk

Section 1

In the following questions, move one letter from the first word to the second word without rearranging the letters to make two new words. These two new words must make sense. Write down the letter and two new words on the line provided.

Example

pine   widow   _____

Answer

n   (The two new words are **pie** and **window**.)

Question 1

tone   fed

Answer: _____

Question 2

there   burn

Answer: _____

Question 3

thrown   bid

Answer: _____

Question 4

scarf   ate

Answer: _____

Question 5

tablet   angle

Answer: _____

Question 6

truck   lean

Answer: _____

Question 7

spend   eel

Answer: _____

Question 8

blame   low

Answer: _____

Question 9

wheat   here

Answer: _____

Question 10

trend   time

Answer: _____

Section 2

In the following questions, four of the five words in each group are related in some way. Underline the word which is the "odd one out".

Example

white	red	keyboard	pink	black

Answer

keyboard

Question 11

tiny	small	huge	massive	weak

Question 12

root	wolf	food	soon	tool

Question 13

slow	inactive	sluggish	indolent	swift

Question 14

witty	smart	clever	person	bright

Question 15

aunt	father	daughter	niece	sister

Question 16

wipe	sow	top	hit	win

Question 17

kite	rectangle	square	trapezium	hexagon

Question 18

two	five	three	four	seven

Section 3

In the following questions, a four letter word is hidden at the end of one word and the beginning of the next word. Underline the pair of words that contains the hidden word.

Example

All the cakes have been eaten.

Answer

been eaten(The hidden word is **neat**.)

Question 19

Bob acknowledged the work of others.

Question 20

Grandma deliberately didn't tell him.

Question 21

This is the brief action plan.

Question 22

Jeff illegally downloaded this music.

Question 23

His father stopped the car.

Question 24

The company ordered the bus yesterday.

Question 25

What sound card do you have?

Question 26

He had an apple and a banana.

Question 27

Is Lisa very upset?

Question 28

You need to think independently.

Question 29

He had a knee dislocation after the football match.

Question 30

They are men's watches.

Section 4

In the questions below, there are two groups of three words. The middle word of each group is formed the same way from the left and right words. Work out the missing word in the second group and write it in the bracket.

Example

hind	(	hand	)	eat
tine	(		)	son

Answer

tone

Question 31

beet	(	bach	)	each
find	(		)	sort

Question 32

ready	(	deep	)	wipe
words	(		)	rose

Question 33

feel	(	long	)	gone
half	(		)	ears

Question 34

about	(	bid	)	find
wheat	(		)	tint

Question 35

vend	(	view	)	wipe
want	(		)	hits

Section 5

In the following questions, letters stand for numbers. Calculate each sum and write down the answer as a letter on the line provided.

Example

If A=5, B=4, C=2, D=3 and E=8, then

A - B + C =_____

Answer

D

Question 36

If A=3, B=2, C=0, D=6 and E=5, find the answer to

this sum and write it as a letter.

(A+B) × C + D= _____

Question 37

If A=42, B=7, C=1, D=2 and E=5, then

A ÷ B + C - D=_____

Question 38

If A=54, B=2, C=3, D=4 and E=9, then

A ÷ E - D=_____

Question 39

If A=1, B=5, C=3, D=21 and E=15, then

(A + B) × C - E=_____

Question 40

If A=2, B=12, C=3, D=9 and E=6,then

(B - E) ÷ A + D =_____

Question 41

If A=6, B=2, C=8, D=4 and E=60, then

$(D + E) \div C - B = $ _____

Question 42

If A=4, B=12, C=10, D=6 and E=8, then

$E + D - A = $ _____

Question 43

If A=60, B=2, C=1, D=4 and E=12, then

$A \div E - D = $ _____

Question 44

If A=8, B=1, C=4, D=5 and E=3, then

$A \times B - D = $ _____

Question 45

If A=5, B=48, C=6, D=3 and E=6, then

$B \div C + D - E = $ _____

Question 46

If A=6, B=20, C=10, D=5 and E=15, then

$A \times D - C - E = $ _____

Section 6

Work out the answer to each question using the given information.

Question 47

Lucy is 6 years older than Lihi who is 4 years younger than Nancy.

How much younger is Nancy than Lucy?

Answer:_____

Question 48

Helena, Laura, Charlotte and Lisa are friends.

Only Laura and Lisa like swimming.

Helena and Laura like playing tennis.

Charlotte and Lisa like playing table tennis but not tennis.

Who likes swimming but not tennis?

Answer:_____

Section 7

In the following questions, the pairs of letters are related in the same way. Use the alphabet shown below to work out the missing letters. Write down the answer on the line provided.

A B C D E F G H I J K L M N O P Q R S T U V W X Y Z

Example

AH is to BI as SW is to _____

Answer

TX

Question 49

BD is to YW as AC is to _____

Question 50

TX is to SY as JK is to _____

Question 51

DF is to EG as YZ is to _____

Question 52

QU is to OS as CA is to _____

Question 53

WE is to YC as UZ is to _____

Question 54

SS is to UW as HH is to _____

Question 55

MN is to LL as FH is to _____

A B C D E F G H I J K L M N O P Q R S T U V W X Y Z

Question 56

TM is to RJ as XY is to _____

Question 57

CG is to DJ as KO is to _____

Section 8

In the following questions, find two words, one from each group, that make a new word when combined. The word from the left group must come first. Underline these two words.

Example

(go	mast	win)
(er	toe	dew)

Answer

mast	er	(The new word is **master**.)

Question 58

(use	to	let)
(full	get	less)

Question 59

(seat	car	for)
(see	belt	boot)

Question 60

(go	put	water)
(through	tip	melon)

Question 61

(birth	hope	go)
(least	mark	over)

Question 62

(in	take	back)
(on	too	dependent)

Question 63

    (over   push   mud)

    (stick   cast   down)

Question 64

    (ever   but   speak)

    (year   on   lasting)

Question 65

    (all   tall   under)

    (right   stand   man)

Question 66

    (proof   fone   say)

    (read   book   it)

Question 67

    (write   fly   count)

    (down   off   away)

Question 68

    (find   back   steam)

    (out   less   ward)

Question 69

    (fight   run   lay)

    (out   buck   dull)

Question 70

    (hedge   wide   upper)

    (narrow   hog   down)

Section 9

In the following questions, write down the number that continues the sequence.

Example

      1   3   5   7   9   _____

Answer

      11

Question 71

      3   7   11   15   19   23   _____

Question 72

      1   2   3   5   8   _____

Question 73

      1   4   9   16   25   36   _____

Question 74

      100   96   92   88   84   80   _____

Question 75

      1   2   4   7   11   16   _____

Question 76

      1   2   4   8   16   _____

Question 77

      48   47   45   42   38   _____

Question 78

      1.5   1.75   2   2.25 2.5   _____

Question 79

     0   3   6   9   12   _____

Question 80

     100   95   90   85   80   75   _____

Question 81

     99   90   81   72   63   _____

Question 82

     0.1   0.3   0.5   0.7   0.9   1.1   _____

Section 10

A B C D E F G H I J K L M N O P Q R S T U V W X Y Z

In the following questions, words and codes are related in some way. Use the alphabet to help you work out the answer to each question.

Example

If the code for **SWAN** is **TYDR**.

What is the code for **TOOL**?

Answer

UQRP

Question 83

If the code for **SCHOOL** is **TDIPPM**.

What is the code for **HOMEWORK**?

Answer: _____

Question 84

If **XNSQZ** means **WORRY**.

What does **UHNDT** mean?

Answer: _____

Question 85

If the code for **ACTION** is **ZAQEJH**.

What is the code for **DOME**?

Answer: _____

A B C D E F G H I J K L M N O P Q R S T U V W X Y Z

Question 86

If the code for **RIVER** is **IREVI**.

What is the code for **ACTED**?

Answer: _____

Question 87

If the code for **NORMAL** is **LMPKYJ**.

What does **AFGAICL** mean?

Answer: _____

Question 88

If the code for **STREAM** is **TVSGBO**.

What is the code for **THOUGH**?

Answer: _____

Question 89

If the code for **MARKET** is **KYPICR**.

What does **NJCYQC** mean?

Answer: _____

Question 90

If the code for **HERE** is **GGOI**.

What is the code for **THERE**?

Answer: _____

Section 11

In the following questions, the three numbers in each group are related in the same way. Find the number that fits in the last group in the same way as the first two groups. Write down your answer in the bracket.

Example

(4[9]5)   (11[13]2)

(3[   ]11)

Answer

14

Question 91

(2[11]4)   (6[33]5)

(3[   ]12)

Question 92

(42[8]6)   (40[6]8)

(10[   ]2)

Question 93

(4[24]8)   (6[26]7)

(6[   ]9)

Question 94

(20[30]5)   (16[18]7)

(30[   ]20)

Question 95

(3[20]7)   (4[35]9)

(6[   ]8)

Question 96

(39[3]13)   (50[10]5)

(24[   ]6)

Question 97

(120[12]10)   (500[100]5)

(54[   ]6)

Question 98

(6[12]2)   (3[45]15)

(10[   ]0.8)

Question 99

(14[50]36)   (27[42]15)

(43[   ]8)

Question 100

(0.5[1.1]0.6)   (2.4[5]2.6)

(11[   ]0.6)

11+ Verbal Reasoning

Standard Practice Paper
Pack Three 11C

Fill in your details:

Name...

Date of birth..

Male ☐   Female ☐

School..

Today's date..

Read these instructions before you start:

- You have **50 minutes** to complete this paper.
- There are 100 **questions** in this paper and each question is worth one mark.
- You may work out your answers in rough using the space around the questions.
- Make sure you write the answers very **clearly**.
- You will not lose marks for crossing out.
- Work as quickly and carefully as you can.
- If you find a question difficult, do **NOT** spend too much time on it but move on to the next one.

Moon Tuition
making the most of your potential

www.moontuition.co.uk

Section 1

In the following questions, move one letter from the first word to the second word without rearranging the letters to make two new words. These two new words must make sense. Write down the letter and two new words on the line provided.

Example

pine   widow   ————————

Answer

n   (The two new words are **pie** and **window**.)

Question 1

know   not

Answer: ————————————

Question 2

care   one

Answer: ————————————

Question 3

farm   lower

Answer: ————————————

Question 4

sting   sun

Answer: ————————————

Question 5

spit   end

Answer: _____

Question 6

bend   bar

Answer: _____

Question 7

rice   though

Answer: _____

Question 8

hold   east

Answer: _____

Question 9

grow   hue

Answer: _____

Question 10

ever   live

Answer: _____

Section 2

In the following questions, three of the five words in each group are related in some way. Underline the two words which are the "odd ones out".

Example

white	red	keyboard	mouse	black

Answer

keyboard	mouse

Question 11

huge	minute	sudden	tiny	pink

Question 12

infer	teacher	conclude	learner	guess

Question 13

nimble	weak	quick	fear	agile

Question 14

bold	fearful	brave	courageous	still

Question 15

spot	blot	tight	metal	stain

Question 16

rectangle	cylinder	cube	kite	square

Question 17

hasty	playing	running	speedy	hurried

Question 18

messy	earth	sun	disordered	untidy

Section 3

In the following questions, a four letter word is hidden at the end of one word and the beginning of the next word. Underline the pair of words that contains the hidden word.

Example

All the cakes have been eaten.

Answer

been eaten(The hidden word is **neat**.)

Question 19

The mining operations could generate huge plumes of sediment.

Question 20

Research into seabed minerals has a long history.

Question 21

This was set up to encourage and manage this new sector.

Question 22

We eventually beat team Ealing.

Question 23

Cisco designed this data centre.

Question 24

We offer Lea kids' bedroom furniture.

Question 25

You need to pay car tax.

Question 26

The nurse lives very close.

Question 27

Please touch that numb end of the toe.

Question 28

Please be around in 30 minutes.

Section 4

In the following sentences, three consecutive letters are missing from the word in capitals. The three letters spell a proper word without changing the order. Write the missing three-letter word on the line provided.

Example:

Anna **SPED** learning piano last month.

Answer:

TOP (The word in capitals is **STOPPED**.)

Question 29

He always DEDS for more food.

Answer:_____

Question 30

The school has put temporary classrooms on its PGROUND.

Answer:_____

Question 31

What is CRIVE writing?

Answer:_____

Question 32

These are the IMS of London.

Answer:_____

Question 33

Have you been to BUCKING Palace?

Answer:_____

Question 34

Please CONT me if you need help.

Answer:_____

Question 35

The class will ST in half an hour.

Answer:_____

Question 36

Please fasten your TBELT.

Answer:_____

Section 5

In the following questions, letters stand for numbers. Calculate each sum and write down the answer as a letter on the line provided.

Example

If A=5, B=4, C=2, D=3 and E=8, then

A - B + C =_____

Answer

D

Question 37

If A=4, B=2, C=5, D=10 and E=8, then

$(A + C) \times B - E=$_____

Question 38

If A=12, B=8, C=4, D=3 and E=6, then

$(A - C) \div B + D=$_____

Question 39

If A=9, B=0, C=5, D=11 and E=8, then

$(A - C) \times B + E=$_____

Question 40

If A=23, B=15, C=4, D=7 and E=9, then

$(A - B) \div C + D =$_____

Question 41

If A=11, B=10, C=4, D=2 and E=31, then

$(E - A) \div B =$_____

Question 42

If A=32, B=18, C=6, D=20 and E=7, then

A - B + C =_____

Question 43

If A=36, B=3, C=5, D=1 and E=9, then

A ÷ E - D =_____

Question 44

If A=8, B=6, C=40, D=4 and E=10, then

A × B - C - D =_____

Question 45

If A=54, B=13, C=6, D=4 and E=9, then

A ÷ C+ D =_____

Question 46

If A=4, B=0, C=3, D=100 and E=1, then

B × D + E + C =_____

Question 47

If A=100, B=0, C=10, D=24 and E=10, then

A ÷ C - E =_____

Question 48

If A=13, B=1, C=9, D=7 and E=63, then

E ÷ C+ D - B =_____

Question 49

If A=1, B=50, C=5, D=25 and E=30, then

B × A - E + C =_____

Question 50

If A=36, B=2, C=5, D=3 and E=10, then

A ÷ B - E - D =_____

Section 6

Work out the answer to each question using the given information.

Question 51

Alex, Dominic and Conor like playing guitar. Adam, Harvey and Alex like playing piano. Susanna and Lara enjoy playing violin. Who plays more than one music instrument?

Answer:_____

Question 52

Charlotte is $1.63m$ tall. Linda is $3cm$ taller than Charlotte but 2 shorter than Rea. Laura is $5cm$ taller than Charlotte.

Who is the shortest?

Answer:_____

Section 7

In the following questions, the pairs of letters are related in the same way. Use the alphabet shown below to work out the missing letters. Write down the answer on the line provided.

A B C D E F G H I J K L M N O P Q R S T U V W X Y Z

Example

AH is to BI as SW is to _____

Answer

TX

Question 53

AB is to ZY as EF is to _____

Question 54

CC is to YZ as PQ is to _____

Question 55

SR is to QT as VW is to _____

Question 56

CB is to FE as DC is to _____

Question 57

JL is to KM as GI is to _____

Question 58

KL is to NJ as YZ is to _____

Question 59

UV is to SS as QQ is to _____

Question 60

WW is to AS as TA is to _____

Section 8

In the following questions, find two words, one from each group, that make a new word when combined. The word from the left group must come first. Underline these two words.

Example

(go   mast   win)

(er   toe   dew)

Answer

mast   er   (The new word is **master**.)

Question 61

(for   cross   go)

(thou   mind   word)

Question 62

(car   taxi   tour)

(driver   go   get)

Question 63

(eight   dark   inter)

(horse   action   teen)

Question 64

(out   beauty   take)

(full   line   turn)

Question 65

(stand   farm   up)

(yard   down   house)

Question 66

(upper   thought   down)

(side   full   more)

Question 67

(for   wife   opt)

(out   ton   ward)

Question 68

(some   what   time)

(about   line   thing)

Question 69

(awe   right   in)

(som   way   firm)

Question 70

(fore   fear   like)

(less   get   ever)

Question 71

(fur   ever   man)

(like   for   again)

Question 72

(swim   be   now)

(long   pool   days)

Section 9

In the following questions, write down the number that continues the sequence.

Example

1   3   5   7   9   _____

Answer

11

Question 73

4   3   7   10   17   27   _____

Question 74

1   4   7   10   13   16   _____

Question 75

2   100   7   95   12   90   _____

Question 76

1   4   9   16   25   _____

Question 77

125   105   85   65   45   _____

Question 78

1   5   3   7   5   _____

Question 79

18   27   36   45   54   63   _____

Question 80

40   36   32   28   24   _____

Section 10

A B C D E F G H I J K L M N O P Q R S T U V W X Y Z

In the following questions, words and codes are related in some way. Use the alphabet to help you work out the answer to each question.

Example

If the code for **SWAN** is **TYDR**.

What is the code for **TOOL**?

Answer

UQRP

Question 81

If the code for **OXFORD** is **PYGPSE**.

What is the code for **STREET**?

Answer: _____

Question 82

If **FQZLLZQ** means **GRAMMAR**.

What does **RBGNNK** mean?

Answer: _____

Question 83

If the code for **CREDIT** is **EPGBKR**.

What is the code for **CRUNCH**?

Answer: _____

Question 84

If **KYQEI** means **LATIN**.

What does **FPBAF** mean?

Answer: _____

Question 85

If the code for **LICENCE** is **MHDDOBF**.

What is the code for **SWINDON**?

Answer: _____

Section 11

In the following questions, the three numbers in each group are related in the same way. Find the number that fits in the last group in the same way as the first two groups. Write down your answer in the bracket.

Example

(4[9]5)   (11[13]2)

(3[   ]11)

Answer

14

Question 86

(15[19]4)   (7[16]9)

(12[   ]15)

Question 87

(5[40]8)   (7[28]4)

(3[   ]9)

Question 88

(24[8]3)   (32[4]8)

(100[   ]10)

Question 89

(2[6]10)   (2[10]18)

(4[   ]10)

Question 90

(5[22]6)   (3[30]12)

(10[   ]20)

Question 91

(50[30]20)   (40[25]15)

(16[   ]12)

Question 92

(3[22]7)   (4[37]9)

(8[   ]8)

Question 93

(17[20]6)   (9[13]8)

(11[   ]8)

Section 12

In the following questions, find a letter that can fit into both sets of brackets to complete the word before the bracket and begin the word after the bracket.

Example

    mea[   ]able

    rol[   ]ong

Answer

    l

Question 94

    wisdo[   ]eal

    swa[   ]ud   Answer:_____

Question 95

    courag[   ]qual

    dat[   ]nable   Answer:_____

Question 96

    towe[   ]ust

    fu[   ]ubber   Answer:_____

Question 97

    sadnes[   ]tay

    new[   ]outh   Answer:_____

Question 98

    sufficien[   ]utor

    sa[   ]ime   Answer:_____

Question 99

traffi[   ]ent

hecti[   ]are   Answer:_____

Question 100

gloom[   ]et

slim[   ]awn   Answer:_____

11+ Verbal Reasoning

Answer Key for
Standard Practice Papers
Pack Three

Read these instructions before you start marking:

- Only the answers given are allowed.
- One mark should be given for each correct answer.
- Do not deduct marks for the wrong answers.

Moon Tuition
making the most of your potential

www.moontuition.co.uk

Standard VR Practice Paper 11A

1.	s (tow, selection)	26.	here (the receipt)
2.	e (fin, wine)	27.	hall (with all)
3.	o (lose, found)	28.	oven (dove near)
4.	d (excite, drill)	29.	east (tea still)
5.	p (super, top)	30.	away (a way)
6.	o (to, thorough)	31.	quiet, loud
7.	n (tow, flown)	32.	odd, even
8.	l (heath, late)	33.	bold, timid
9.	a (red, coat)	34.	hide, disclose
10.	e (nod, quiet or quite)	35.	vague, clear
11.	river, mountain	36.	C
12.	stalk, root	37.	E
13.	food, bread	38.	D
14.	cloud, earth	39.	D
15.	fierce, wild	40.	E
16.	superior, size	41.	C
17.	force, meet	42.	A
18.	merry, structure	43.	B
19.	done (found one)	44.	A
20.	fore (for eggs)	45.	E
21.	down (widow never)	46.	D
22.	dent (hidden the)	47.	Jack
23.	ally (All yellow)	48.	One
24.	cake (Jessica keeps)	49.	QZ
25.	hero (her old)	50.	EZ

51.	BS	76.	over
52.	ON	77.	sector
53.	MV	78.	NPSF
54.	WD	79.	SUGAR
55.	ZB	80.	YKCLB
56.	QR	81.	SKYIW
57.	TIE	82.	PAPER
58.	CAP	83.	SINVFI
59.	GET	84.	ORANGE
60.	BED	85.	SFTVMU
61.	FOR	86.	90
62.	21	87.	7
63.	96	88.	40
64.	5	89.	30
65.	16	90.	12
66.	65	91.	25
67.	17	92.	42
68.	2.5	93.	24
69.	40	94.	e
70.	36	95.	l
71.	8	96.	t
72.	32	97.	s
73.	head	98.	f
74.	mate	99.	p
75.	buy	100.	m

Standard VR Practice Paper 11B

1. e (ton, feed) or n (toe, fend)
2. t (here, burnt)
3. n (throw, bind)
4. f (scar, fate)
5. t (table, tangle)
6. r (tuck, learn) or t (ruck, leant)
7. p (send, peel) or s (pend, seel)
8. b (blame, blow)
9. w (heat, where)
10. r (tend, timer)
11. weak
12. wolf
13. swift
14. person
15. father
16. wipe
17. hexagon
18. four
19. back (Bob acknowledge)
20. made (Grandma deliberately)
21. fact (brief action)
22. fill (Jeff illegally)
23. hers (father stopped)
24. busy (bus yesterday)
25. hats (What sound)

26. lean or plea (apple and)
27. save (Lisa very)
28. kind (think independently)
29. need (knee dislocation)
30. swat (men's watches)
31. fort
32. does
33. fare
34. hit
35. wish
36. D
37. E
38. B
39. C
40. B
41. A
42. C
43. C
44. E
45. A
46. D
47. 2 years younger
48. Lisa
49. ZX
50. IL

51.	ZA	76.	32
52.	AY	77.	33
53.	WX	78.	2.75
54.	JL	79.	15
55.	EF	80.	70
56.	VV	81.	54
57.	LR	82.	1.3
58.	useless	83.	IPNFXPSL
59.	seatbelt	84.	TIMES
60.	watermelon	85.	CMJA
61.	birthmark	86.	ZXGVW
62.	independent	87.	CHICKEN
63.	overcast	88.	UJPWHJ
64.	everlasting	89.	PLEASE
65.	understand	90.	SJBVZ
66.	proofread	91.	39
67.	countdown	92.	6
68.	backward	93.	30
69.	layout	94.	20
70.	hedgehog	95.	47
71.	27	96.	4
72.	13	97.	9
73.	49	98.	8
74.	76	99.	51
75.	22	100.	11.6

Standard VR Practice Paper 11C

1. k (now, knot)
2. c (are, once or cone)
3. f (arm, flower)
4. t (sing, stun)
5. s (pit, send)
6. n (bed, barn) or b (end, barb)
7. r (ice, through)
8. l (hod, least)
9. g (row, huge)
10. r (eve, liver)
11. sudden, pink
12. teacher, learner
13. weak, fear
14. fearful, still
15. tight, metal
16. cylinder, cube
17. playing, running
18. earth, sun
19. them (The mining)
20. chin or hint (Research into)
21. news (new sector)
22. meal (team Ealing)
23. code (Cisco designed)
24. leak (Lea kids')
25. cart (car tax)
26. then (The nurse)
27. bend (numb end)
28. bear (be around)
29. man
30. lay
31. eat
32. age
33. ham
34. act
35. art or tar
36. sea
37. D
38. C
39. E
40. E
41. D
42. D
43. B
44. D
45. B
46. A
47. B
48. A
49. D
50. C

51.	Alex	76.	36
52.	Charlotte	77.	25
53.	VU	78.	9
54.	LN	79.	72
55.	TY	80.	20
56.	GF	81.	TUSFFU
57.	HJ	82.	SCHOOL
58.	BX	83.	EPWLEF
59.	ON	84.	GREEK
60.	XW	85.	TVJMENO
61.	crossword	86.	27
62.	cargo	87.	27
63.	interaction	88.	10
64.	outline	89.	7
65.	farmhouse or farmyard	90.	60
66.	downside	91.	4
67.	forward	92.	65
68.	something or timeline	93.	15
69.	infirm	94.	m
70.	fearless	95.	e
71.	manlike	96.	r
72.	belong	97.	s
73.	44	98.	t
74.	19	99.	c
75.	17	100.	y

Printed in Great Britain
by Amazon